Happy Holidays!
Memorial Day

by Rebecca Sabelko

BELLWETHER MEDIA
MINNEAPOLIS, MN

Blastoff! Beginners are developed by literacy experts and educators to meet the needs of early readers. These engaging informational texts support young children as they begin reading about their world. Through simple language and high frequency words paired with crisp, colorful photos, Blastoff! Beginners launch young readers into the universe of independent reading.

Sight Words in This Book 🔍

are	in	now	play	we
day	is	of	red	who
for	it	on	the	
go	many	out	they	
have	may	people	to	

This edition first published in 2024 by Bellwether Media, Inc.

No part of this publication may be reproduced in whole or in part without written permission of the publisher. For information regarding permission, write to Bellwether Media, Inc., Attention: Permissions Department, 6012 Blue Circle Drive, Minnetonka, MN 55343.

Library of Congress Cataloging-in-Publication Data

LC record for Memorial Day available at: https://lccn.loc.gov/2023001665

Text copyright © 2024 by Bellwether Media, Inc. BLASTOFF! BEGINNERS and associated logos are trademarks and/or registered trademarks of Bellwether Media, Inc.

Editor: Christina Leaf   Designer: Laura Sowers

Printed in the United States of America, North Mankato, MN.

Table of Contents

It Is Memorial Day	4
A Day to Honor	6
A Day to Remember	12
Memorial Day Facts	22
Glossary	23
To Learn More	24
Index	24

It Is Memorial Day

Families lay flowers on **graves**.
It is Memorial Day.

A Day to Honor

Memorial Day is the last Monday in May.

Many people call it the start of summer!

We honor **fallen soldiers**. They fought to keep the U.S. free.

A Day to Remember

People visit graves.
They leave flowers.
They put out flags.

Many people wear red flowers. They honor people who died.

People go to **parades**.
They fly the flag.

parade

Summer begins!
People have
picnics.
They play games.

Many soldiers fought for us. Now we are free!

Memorial Day Facts

Celebrating Memorial Day

grave • flag • flowers

Memorial Day Activities

visit graves

go to parades

have picnics

Glossary

fallen soldiers

people who fought and died for their country

graves

places where people are laid to rest after they die

parades

people or groups who walk together during events

picnics

outside parties with food

To Learn More

ON THE WEB

FACTSURFER

Factsurfer.com gives you a safe, fun way to find more information.

1. Go to www.factsurfer.com.

2. Enter "Memorial Day" into the search box and click 🔍.

3. Select your book cover to see a list of related content.

Index

families, 4
flags, 12, 16
flowers, 4, 12, 14
free, 10, 20
games, 18
graves, 4, 5, 12
May, 6
Monday, 6

parades, 16, 17
picnics, 18, 19
soldiers, 10, 20
summer, 8, 18
U.S., 10

The images in this book are reproduced through the courtesy of: Bill Chizek, front cover; paulaphoto, p. 3; jarenwicklund, pp. 4-5; Monkey Business Images, pp. 6-7, 22 (have picnics); Deborah Kolb, pp. 8-9; Inge Johnsson/ Alamy, pp. 10-11; magicoven, p. 12; Christinlola, pp. 12-13; Stephanie Murton, p. 14; SOPA Images/ Alamy, pp. 14-15; Vsevolod33, pp. 16-17; Travelpixs, pp. 18-19; BDphoto, pp. 20-21; Yobro10, p. 22; Tim Brown/ Alamy, p. 22 (visit graves); oberto Galan, p. 22 (go to parades); Leena Robinson, p. 23 (fallen soldiers); Denise Lett, p. 23 (graves); EAGiven, p. 23 (parades;); New Africa, p. 23 (picnics).